THEODORE ROOSEVELT'S
★ PRESIDENCY ★

THEODORE ROOSEVELT'S
PRESIDENCY

HEATHER E. SCHWARTZ

LERNER PUBLICATIONS ◆ MINNEAPOLIS

Lerner Publications Company
A division of Lerner Publishing Group, Inc.
241 First Avenue North
Minneapolis, MN 55401 USA

For reading levels and more information, look up this title at www.lernerbooks.com.

Main body text set in Caecilia LT Std 9.5/15.
Typeface provided by Adobe Systems.

Library of Congress Cataloging-in-Publication Data

Names: Schwartz, Heather E.
Title: Theodore Roosevelt's presidency / by Heather E. Schwartz.
Description: Minneapolis, MN : Lerner Publications, 2015. | Series: Presidential powerhouses
Identifiers: LCCN 2015000945| ISBN 9781467779302 (lb : alk. paper) | ISBN 9781467786010 (eb pdf)
Subjects: LCSH: Roosevelt, Theodore, 1858–1919—Juvenile literature. | United States—Politics and government—1901–1909—Juvenile literature. | Presidents—United States—Biography—Juvenile literature.
Classification: LCC E756 .S393 2015 | DDC 973.91/1092—dc23

LC record available at http://lccn.loc.gov/2015000945

Manufactured in the United States of America
1 – VP – 7/15/16

★ TABLE OF CONTENTS ★

★ INTRODUCTION ★

Theodore Roosevelt had been vice president of the United States for only six months when he received shocking news. On September 6, 1901, while at a luncheon in Vermont, he learned an assassin had shot President William McKinley in the stomach and chest during a visit to western New York. As second in command, Roosevelt needed to travel to Buffalo, New York, as quickly as possible.

President William McKinley was shot by Leon Czolgosz (holding cloth-covered gun near center) on September 6, 1901.

Once there, however, Roosevelt found the president appeared to be doing well. Doctors expected McKinley to make a full recovery. To keep the country from panicking, Roosevelt's advisers urged him to leave. He headed to New York's Adirondack Mountains, more than 200 miles (320 kilometers) away, for a vacation. His wife Edith and their children joined him there.

But during a hike he received a telegram about McKinley's condition. The president was dying. The telegram asked Roosevelt to return to Buffalo immediately.

At first, Roosevelt wasn't sure if he should rush. The news was difficult to believe. Roosevelt had so recently visited and found the president recovering. Then a second telegram stated that McKinley's situation was dire. Roosevelt was convinced—there was no time to waste.

A HARROWING JOURNEY

By the time Roosevelt started out for Buffalo, it was close to midnight on September 13. The mountainous roads were dark and slippery. For the first leg of his journey, he traveled for hours by wagon to the nearest train station 35 miles (56 km) away. The distance was too far for a single set of horses. In fact, the strain was so great that Roosevelt switched wagons three times. Each time, a new driver and horses continued the trip.

It was early morning when Roosevelt finally reached the train station in North Creek, New York. His secretary, William Loeb Jr., met him there with a telegram. Roosevelt learned that the president had died at a quarter past two in the morning. The news meant Roosevelt would soon become the next president.

The trials of his trip were not behind him yet. Boarding a train, Roosevelt set off through dense fog. There was a crash and a short delay when the train hit a handcar. In Albany, New York's capital,

EDISON'S X-RAY

After President William McKinley was shot, inventor Thomas Edison sent doctors a newly developed medical device—an X-ray machine. Edison thought it might help find a stray bullet doctors could not locate within McKinley's body. Doctors, however, refused to use it. They were concerned it would be dangerous to move the president. While they believed he was recovering, McKinley developed a deadly infection. Finding the bullet would not have saved him.

he had to switch to another train for the rest of the journey. More than twelve hours after the start of his trip, Roosevelt finally reached his destination.

After an exhausting journey, there was little time for rest. In Buffalo, Roosevelt ate a quick lunch and borrowed formal clothing from Ansley Wilcox, a friend in the city. First, Roosevelt paid his respects to McKinley, whose body was lying in state. Then, back at Wilcox's mansion home, Roosevelt was sworn into office as president of the United States on September 14. Only forty-three people watched Roosevelt take the presidential oath of office. These witnesses included news reporters, cabinet members, and local dignitaries.

THE TWENTY-SIXTH PRESIDENT

By the time Roosevelt became president, he had a reputation for being many things—a hunter, a naturalist, an author, a reformer, a cowboy, a family man, and a military hero. He was an influential leader who could take the country where he wanted it to go.

On his path to the presidency, Roosevelt took many detours in both his personal and professional life. Those detours strengthened his spirit, built his character, and informed his future decisions. Tragic circumstances had landed him in the nation's highest office. But as the twenty-sixth US president, Roosevelt was both prepared and determined to serve his country well.

Theodore Roosevelt is sworn in as president at the Wilcox home in Buffalo, New York, on September 14, 1901.

★ CHAPTER ONE ★

ROOSEVELT'S EARLY YEARS

When Theodore, called Teedie by some, was a child, few people would have predicted he'd ever become president of the United States. Born in New York City, New York, on October 27, 1858, Theodore was sickly as a youngster. He suffered from asthma, allergies, and digestive ailments. He wasn't expected to live long. As he grew older, he also showed a timid side to his personality and suffered from recurring nightmares.

Theodore wasn't strong as a child, but he was born with advantages in life. His family was close, supportive, socially prominent, and wealthy. His father, Theodore Roosevelt Sr., was his son's hero who helped Theodore breathe during life-threatening asthma attacks. "I could breathe, I could sleep, when he held me in his arms. My father—he got me breath, he got me lungs, strength—life," Roosevelt later said.

Theodore's father set a compelling example for his children as a vigorous, healthy man with solid moral principles and strong leadership skills. His father was a philanthropist who believed in using his wealth and position to help others. His contributions to society included working to establish New York City's Children's Aid Society, the New York Orthopedic Hospital, the American

Museum of Natural History, and the American Museum of Art. He helped others in personal ways too. The elder Roosevelt once organized a dinner for his wealthy friends and surprised them by including disabled children as guests. He then asked his friends to contribute money to benefit the children.

Theodore Roosevelt Sr. was a successful businessman in New York City.

Theodore's mother, Martha "Mittie" Bulloch, was a romantic, eccentric, and charming southern belle who greatly influenced her son's development and personality. His mother had an allegiance to the South before, during, and after the American Civil War (1861–1865). Because of his wife's loyalties to the South, the elder Roosevelt had not enlisted in the US military to fight for the North during the war. He stayed out of the North-South battle at Mittie's request. She didn't want to see her husband at war against her family still living in the South. As wealthy men often did at the time, her husband chose the legal option to pay a substitute to fight for him. This disappointed Theodore, who otherwise adored his father. He believed in his father's strength and thought that avoiding war seemed cowardly. Later in life, Roosevelt echoed his thoughts on cowardly behavior and the will to fight, stating: "Cowardice in a race, as in an individual, is the unpardonable sin . . . No triumph of peace is quite so great as the supreme triumphs of war."

GROWING UP ROOSEVELT

As a boy, Theodore, whose asthma prevented him from much physical activity, was a voracious reader. He was especially drawn to books about great adventures and read many books from his family's library. One of the first books he loved was David Livingstone's *Missionary Travels and Researches in South Africa*, which contained beautiful illustrations of exotic animals and birds.

Theodore was also a born naturalist. The young Roosevelt collected frogs, birds, mice, and snakes. He stuffed and sketched many of his findings. He kept detailed records too, including information about each animal's sex, location, size, and stomach contents. In 1867, when he was nine years old, Theodore even started a home museum, naming it the Roosevelt Museum of Natural History. From his collection of specimens, he later donated several items to the American Museum of Natural History that his father had cofounded.

Throughout his childhood, Theodore continued to suffer from asthma and nightmares. At the time, medical treatments for asthma were very primitive and did not help. They included using coffee, tobacco, and ipecac (a drug to induce vomiting). Watching their son suffer from the constant attacks terrified the Roosevelts,

As a child, Theodore was often in poor health.

who feared for Theodore's life. Theodore's father urged the boy to try to improve his health through exercise, stating: "You have the mind but not the body, and without the help of the body the mind cannot go as far as it should. You *must* make your body." The family built a gym in their New York City home for all four Roosevelt children to use.

Theodore fought to become the strong man he wanted to be. While building his mind through reading and other creative pursuits, he also worked hard to overcome his physical challenges. Theodore spent almost all of his spare time in the gym exercising, proving to himself and his family that he could overcome his physical frailties. For years, Theodore worked with steady determination to strengthen his body through exercise. He took boxing lessons and went hiking with his father.

FAMILY LIFE

Theodore grew up with three siblings: older sister, Anna (called Bamie), younger brother, Elliott, and younger sister, Corinne. They were educated by private tutors. They also all used their home gym, as each had health problems to overcome. Roosevelt remained close to his sisters and brother throughout his life. Two of Roosevelt's relatives watched his presidency closely. Franklin Delano Roosevelt was Theodore's younger cousin by twenty-four years. Eleanor Roosevelt was Theodore's niece, daughter of his brother, Elliott. Franklin and Eleanor married in 1905, and Franklin was elected president in 1933.

Theodore's health was improving, so in 1871, when he was twelve years old, his parents allowed him to take a camping trip to the Adirondack Mountains. It was one of many places he visited to collect natural specimens, study birds, and cultivate his lifelong love of nature. Then his father discovered Theodore was nearsighted. With glasses, Theodore was no longer clumsy. He later recalled, "I had no idea how beautiful the world was until I got those spectacles." He could shoot targets accurately now too. On a family trip to Egypt and Syria, he took advantage of his improved sight by shooting several hundred birds, some of which were later displayed in his museum.

By the time he left home for Harvard University at the age of seventeen, Theodore was ready to prove himself in the world. In

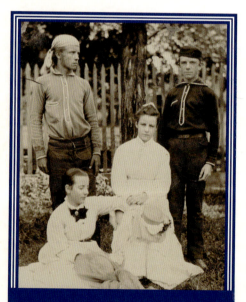

Theodore (back left) with his brother, Elliott, sister Corinne (center), and childhood friend Edith Carow in 1875

college he studied natural history and thrived as an industrious student with a strict daily schedule and busy social life. But he suffered a tragedy too. During his second year, his father died at the age of forty-six soon after being diagnosed with cancer. Roosevelt was devastated that he was not there to say good-bye to his father. On February 12, 1878, Roosevelt wrote in his diary, "He has just been buried . . . With the help of my God I will try to lead such a life as he would have wished."

At home, Roosevelt turned to his childhood friend Edith Carow for comfort. They seemed destined to marry until an argument drove them apart. Neither ever told anyone what had happened between them.

Roosevelt returned to school with determination and energy. He joined clubs; started writing his first book, *The Naval War of 1812*; and fought in the school's boxing championship.

He also met a classmate's cousin, Alice Hathaway Lee, fell in love, and resolved to marry her. Lee was in no rush to marry Roosevelt though, having many admirers to choose from. Roosevelt intensely pursued Lee, who was surprised at his tenacity. She kept him in her life as a friend, but Lee's friend later recalled that she "had no intention of marrying him . . ." Lee gave Roosevelt the slightest amount of hope, though, and he continued to pursue her.

The two eventually started a courtship, and Roosevelt proposed to Lee on June 20, 1879. She refused, but Roosevelt did not lose his resolve. Eight months after his first proposal, Roosevelt asked Lee again. In his diary on January 25, 1880, Roosevelt wrote, "At last everything is settled; but it seems impossible to realize it . . . after much pleading my own sweet, pretty darling consented to be my wife." It had taken years, but Roosevelt had finally won Lee's heart.

Alice Hathaway Lee became engaged to Roosevelt in early 1880.

MARRIAGE AND CAREER

In 1880 Roosevelt graduated from Harvard University and began attending Columbia Law School. That year he and Lee married. They made plans to build their dream house in Oyster Bay, New York. Together, they enjoyed life as part of high society, attending dinner parties, galas, and other affairs.

In 1881 Roosevelt dropped out of law school to begin a career in politics. It was an unusual choice at that time for a wealthy and prominent member of high society. He was soon elected as the youngest member of the New York State Assembly. Around this time he also donated the contents of the Roosevelt Museum of Natural History to the Smithsonian Institution, in Washington, DC. It included insects and 250 bird and mammal specimens.

Working in Albany, New York, Roosevelt used his position to fight corruption and quickly gained a reputation as a tough politician. In 1882 he visited cigar workers on the Lower East Side of New York City to see their lives up close. He was horrified to see workers in such poverty. Coming from his privileged upbringing, Roosevelt was sheltered from the conditions facing the working class. His visits to the cigar factories strengthened his resolve to fight for a bill to protect cigar workers. Although the bill was later struck down, it was one example of Roosevelt's dedication to using politics to help people.

By 1883 Roosevelt's career was taking off. With a baby on the way, his personal life was also thriving. On February 12, 1884, his wife gave birth to the couple's daughter, Alice Lee Roosevelt, in New York City. It should have been a happy time. The joyous event, however, was soon followed by tragedies that would alter the course of Roosevelt's life. Two days after the birth, on February 14, Roosevelt's mother, Mittie, died

of typhoid fever at the age of forty-eight. Only hours later, his wife Alice died of Bright's disease, a kidney disorder. The disease had not been detected through her pregnancy but had been exacerbated by it. She was twenty-two years old when she died.

After his mother and wife died so unexpectedly, Roosevelt's world fell apart. In his diary that day, he wrote a large black X and a single sentence, "The light has gone out of my life."

THE INDUSTRIAL REVOLUTION

The Industrial Revolution, which began in the late eighteenth century and lasted for more than a century, brought mechanized processes to factories in the United States and other parts of the world. Workers did not have to be as highly skilled as they once had to be. This was the beginning of what would become a large labor force of unskilled workers in the United States. These workers weren't protected from employers who paid them little, required long hours, and often provided poor working conditions. Many new immigrants were desperate for jobs and accepted the conditions because they had no other employment choices. Children could work at any age—and had to in order to support their families. Many children worked in factories on machines that could cut off hands or fingers. In the late nineteenth century, workers were tired of unfair employers and dangerous working conditions. Many formed unions to protect their rights and earn fair wages.

STARTING OVER

Distraught over his losses, Roosevelt left his new baby with his sister Bamie. He left his home and his career in politics to move to the Dakota Territory, in present-day North Dakota and South Dakota. The land there had recently been taken from American Indian tribes by the US government and redistributed to US citizens, which did not include American Indians. This US policy was designed to break up tribal governments and power, and it was a policy that Roosevelt would later publicly support.

When Roosevelt arrived in the Dakota Territory in 1884, he started a new life raising cattle on a small ranch he'd purchased with money inherited from his father. He vowed never again to speak of his wife. At the age of twenty-four, he also decided to honor her memory by never marrying again.

As a New York City native, Roosevelt didn't immediately fit in with the rougher men of the West. His spurs, belt buckles, and guns were fancy and expensive. He wore a costly tailor-made fringed shirt. He spoke like the upper-class citizen he was, using expressions and grammar uncommon among the cowboys he met.

Roosevelt moved to the Dakota Territory to start a cattle ranch in 1884.

"CIVILIZING" AMERICAN INDIANS

Roosevelt believed that American Indians should abandon their tribal ways and adopt the "civilized" ways of American society. This was a common belief among many white Americans who wanted to expand into lands occupied by American Indian tribes. This "civilizing" included adopting the Christian religion, attending white boarding schools, breaking up tribal lands and awarding plots to individuals, and granting US citizenship to American Indians who accepted individual land plots.

Speaking in support of the Dawes Act of 1887, which allowed the US government to break up American Indian land for individuals, Roosevelt made many comments that indicated his opinions of American Indians and their customs. "In my judgment, the time has arrived when we should definitely make up our minds to recognize the Indian as an individual and not as a member of a tribe," he said. "The Indian should be treated as an individual—like the white man."

Roosevelt didn't have the skills they possessed either. He wasn't the best shot with his gun or a talented rider, but he was determined to earn his place as a cowboy. He showed grit, riding in all kinds of weather and tackling the difficult physical work of rounding up cattle. His tenacity earned him respect. During the next two years, Roosevelt transformed himself into a cowboy and grew stronger in body and spirit.

Throughout his time in the West, Roosevelt made trips back to New York to visit his daughter and the rest of his family.

On those trips, he carefully tried to avoid meeting with his childhood sweetheart, Edith Carow. He didn't want to risk falling in love again, feeling it would be disloyal to his late wife. But Carow was a longtime family friend, and eventually Roosevelt encountered her again. Once back in touch, they started seeing each other secretly and soon became engaged.

Roosevelt and Carow married on December 2, 1886. Just after the honeymoon, 60 percent of his cattle herd in the Dakota Territory was killed during a terrible winter that lasted into 1887. His financial losses totaled $20,000, and Roosevelt's ranch business was destroyed. It was time to start over again.

The couple made their home in Oyster Bay. They named their house Sagamore Hill. The couple brought Roosevelt's daughter Alice to live with them, and they eventually had five children together.

In the early days of his second marriage, Roosevelt wrote four books about hunting, politics, and the West. Before marrying Edith, he ran for mayor of New York City and lost, but he was ready to return to politics. When Benjamin Harrison ran for president in 1888, Roosevelt picked up his political career again by campaigning for him.

RISING REFORMER

When Harrison won the presidential election, he appointed Roosevelt as the country's civil service commissioner. It was Roosevelt's job to eliminate the rampant corruption among federal officials. He made sure they were qualified for their positions and weren't simply handed their jobs as paybacks for votes.

Roosevelt had no problem taking on the corrupt system. When he fired those who didn't deserve their jobs, he gained the confidence of the American people. As time went on, he also caught the attention of New York City mayor William Strong, who needed Roosevelt's help cleaning up the corrupt New York City Police Department. In 1895 Strong offered Roosevelt the job of New York City police commissioner, which he accepted.

Before Roosevelt, New York City's police officers were not trained and often weren't qualified. His reforms standardized the weapons they used, so police officers all had the same weapons in good working order. Before that, police officers had used the guns they owned, including shotguns, muskets, revolvers, or other weapons. Roosevelt also made sure officers were trained to use their weapons. Roosevelt stopped common practices among corrupt officers, including sleeping on the job, accepting bribes, and extorting money from local citizens. He enjoyed disguising himself to patrol the streets at night, catching corruption

As commissioner, Roosevelt worked to reform the corrupt practices of the New York City Police Department.

in action. Before he was finished with the position of police commissioner, Roosevelt also created a bike patrol, brought telephones into the precincts, and allowed women and Jewish citizen to work in the department for the first time in history. His changes in the department were revolutionary, as women and Jews were often treated as second-class citizens in the United States at the time.

The media loved Roosevelt the reformer. They followed him around the city and reported on the dramatic changes he was inspiring. He became a well-known character—and cartoon—in newspapers. People started talking about him and speculating about his future. With his fearless, no-nonsense attitude and high moral standards, Roosevelt seemed to have what it took to become an excellent president one day.

Not everyone loved Roosevelt's brand of reform while he was the New York City police commissioner, however, because he enforced all laws equally, whether popular or unpopular. When he made sure saloons obeyed a law prohibiting the sale of alcohol on Sundays, some people became angry and Roosevelt even received letter bombs in the mail.

BOLD LEADER

After leaving his post as the police commissioner, Roosevelt became assistant secretary of the navy under President William McKinley in 1897. He was excited to build a stronger navy for the country and wanted the United States to grow into a world power. Roosevelt saw an opportunity for the United States in Cuba's struggle with Spain. Cuba, a large Caribbean island, was a colony of Spain that was struggling to gain independence.

In 1898 the USS *Maine* battleship was sent to a location off the coast of Cuba, as a show of support for the rebelling colonists. The ship wasn't there long before it exploded and went down.

The USS Maine exploded off the coast of Havana, Cuba, on February 15, 1898.

Initial investigations indicated the explosion happened on board. But reporting on the event inflamed the issue. The trend in newspapers at the time was "yellow journalism." Instead of writing carefully reported facts, newspapers printed sensational stories that stretched and even fabricated the truth. It was a way to entice readers and increase sales, and it also had powerful real-world consequences.

After the explosion, newspapers focused on rumors that Spain might have caused the ship's sinking. While McKinley hesitated to declare war, Roosevelt pushed the issue. When the secretary of the navy was out for the day, Roosevelt became the acting secretary and sent orders to prepare for an attack on a Spanish fleet. Within two months, the United States declared war with Spain, launching the Spanish-American War (April–August 1898).

Excited, Roosevelt wanted to fight in the war more than he wanted to continue as assistant secretary. He left his position to

become a lieutenant colonel in the US Army. He formed a cavalry regiment of one thousand men of varied backgrounds who knew how to ride horses.

Roosevelt's regiment included cowboys, college graduates, sports champions, and American Indians. The media nicknamed them the Rough Riders. The regiment saw combat in Cuba and won two important battles against Spain: the Battle of Las Guasimas and the Battle of San Juan Heights. The war lasted three and a half months, and the strength of the US Navy led to victory. When the conflict ended, the Treaty of Paris gave the United States possession of Guam, Puerto Rico, and the Philippines, which had been under Spanish control. The United States also became the protectorate to Cuba, which meant the United States would control as well as protect the Latin American country. With this treaty, the four-hundred-year Spanish Empire in South America crumbled.

PHILIPPINE–AMERICAN WAR

After the Treaty of Paris granted power over the Philippines to the United States, another war broke out. The Philippines fought for independence from the United States between 1899 and 1902. The United States wanted to control the Philippines to gain opportunities in Asia and prevent another country from taking control. During the conflict, forty-two hundred US soldiers and twenty thousand Filipino soldiers were killed. The United States won the war but eventually recognized the Philippines as an independent nation in 1946.

Roosevelt (left) and his friend Leonard Wood (right) led the Rough Riders during the Spanish-American War.

Although Roosevelt was credited with forming the Rough Riders, his friend and war hero Leonard Wood helped and was colonel of the regiment. Still, Roosevelt was such a popular figure in the United States that the public gave him most of the credit.

For his part in making the country a powerful authority in global affairs, he returned from the war a hero in many people's eyes. He was then more ready than ever for a prominent political role.

★ CHAPTER TWO ★

TAKING
THE
PRESIDENCY

After the Spanish-American War ended in 1898, Roosevelt ran as the Republican candidate for governor of New York. His charm and war hero status easily won him the victory. Once in office, Roosevelt proved he was still a reformer. He passed bills to tax corporations, limit working hours, improve factory conditions, and preserve state forests. While he was governor, he also ended racial segregation in New York schools. He gained support for many of his causes by talking to newspaper journalists and through their news stories.

Roosevelt's politics didn't mesh with those of Senator Thomas Platt, the boss of the New York State Republican Party. Platt hadn't wanted to nominate Roosevelt for governor. At that time, party bosses had great control over delegates and could sway the vote during elections. Platt controlled 700 of the 971 delegates in the state. While Roosevelt wanted the government—and specifically the Republican Party—to take a stronger role in controlling business, Platt was more concerned with business owners' rights. He found Roosevelt difficult to work with because Roosevelt insisted on making independent decisions, even if they went against his party's beliefs. Reluctantly, Platt did finally back Roosevelt, as he seemed to be the likeliest winner among the available candidates.

On November 21, 1899, US vice president Garret A. Hobart died suddenly of heart problems. The office was open, and Platt saw his chance to remove Roosevelt from the governor's office. He helped make sure Roosevelt was nominated as the running mate to President William McKinley, who was running for his second term in 1900. Though Hobart had expanded the office, vice presidents typically had little power. After their service, most did not have political futures. The move was meant to remove Roosevelt from New York and ultimately end his political career.

Roosevelt (center) gives a speech from a railroad car during his 1898 campaign for governor of New York.

THE BOONE & CROCKETT CLUB

As an adult, Roosevelt enjoyed being in the wilderness. In 1887 he revisited the Badlands in the Dakota Territory for a hunting trip. He found the site much changed from when he'd ranched there. Once filled with big game, the area had little wildlife by the late 1800s. The tall grasses were also gone, and the creeks were dry. Roosevelt was concerned about the area's future.

Back in New York, Roosevelt worked with others to form the Boone & Crockett Club. It became an organization focused on preserving large game in the wild as well as forest and land conservation. The club lobbied the government to protect Yellowstone National Park, which was being developed by resort owners. In 1894 Congress approved the Park Protection Act to preserve Yellowstone. Roosevelt would later, as president, continue his conservation work that began with the Boone & Crockett Club.

The Boone & Crockett Club lobbied for the preservation of Yellowstone National Park.

Roosevelt resisted the nomination, believing the vice presidency held no future for his career. He told the *New York Tribune*, "Under no circumstances could I, or would I, accept the nomination for the vice presidency." But many of Roosevelt's friends thought the vice presidency would be a good move for him as it would bring him national attention. They thought Roosevelt might be able to make more of the vice presidential position and even move on to become president. They pushed for Roosevelt's nomination too.

When it came, he accepted the nomination reluctantly. He could see that he didn't really have any choice if he wanted to continue in politics. He couldn't expect to succeed by returning to New York state politics under Platt, so he did all he could to

President William McKinley (left) asked Roosevelt to campaign as his vice president in 1900.

make the most of his new position. As McKinley's running mate, he campaigned diligently. He traveled close to 22,000 miles (35,400 km) and visited twenty-four of the country's forty-five states. He delivered 673 speeches in 567 different towns. His efforts paid off when McKinley won a second term.

McKinley's win was Roosevelt's too, but to Roosevelt, the victory felt like the loss of his career and political aspirations. For six months, he served as McKinley's vice president, and the job didn't require much beyond keeping track of the president's appointments. Roosevelt spent time at Sagamore Hill and considered returning to law school. He went on a trip to Vermont.

MCKINLEY'S DEATH

On September 14, 1901, Polish immigrant Leon Czolgosz shot McKinley in Buffalo, New York. Czolgosz was a Socialist, a person who believes in communal ownership and distribution of goods in a society. He was also an anarchist who rebelled against the government, believing that there should not even be one in the United States. He thought corruption existed within the government and advocated overthrowing it using violent force. After the shooting, McKinley was still conscious and asked his guards not to hurt Czolgosz. The assassin was tried in court and found guilty and then executed in an electric chair on October 29, 1901.

McKinley's death changed Roosevelt's place in politics and history forever. As second in command, Roosevelt assumed power and became the nation's next president. While former first lady Ida McKinley packed her belongings, Roosevelt stayed with his sister Bamie and her family in Washington, DC. On September 23, 1901, Roosevelt spent his first night in the White House. He was forty-two years old when he took over as president—the youngest president the country had ever had.

ANARCHY AND TERRORISM

During the nineteenth century, the anarchist movement gained momentum in the United States. Anarchists believe all forms of government are inherently unjust and evil. They wish to live in a society free from authority and laws. The movement began in Europe and spread to the United States as waves of immigrants came to the country. The anarchist began to represent the needs of the working class, who fought against the tyranny of business owners and the government. A labor force of unskilled workers grew during the Industrial Revolution and the perceived threat of anarchy against the government grew as well. Several bombings and assassination attempts, including McKinley's, made the anarchists' threats very real.

The Haymarket Square Riot was one of the first anarchist events resulting in deaths. On May 4, 1886, in Chicago, Illinois, a peaceful protest for workers' rights had been organized by anarchists. It escalated into a riot when the police tried to disperse the crowd that had gathered. An unknown person threw a bomb, and police began shooting. An estimated eleven to fifteen people were killed and sixty to one hundred people were wounded. The riot sparked a societal panic about immigrants, anarchy, and labor leaders. More terroristic events further spread the fear of anarchy in the United States.

Roosevelt believed anarchists were the most dangerous criminals in the country, stating: "The Anarchist is a criminal whose perverted instincts lead him to prefer confusion and chaos to the most beneficent form of social order . . . The Anarchist is everywhere not merely the enemy of system and of progress, but the deadly foe of liberty."

PRINCESS ALICE

Roosevelt's first child, Alice, became a bit of a rebel as she grew older. She had a strained relationship with her stepmother, Edith, and her father refused to even discuss her mother with Alice. Alice's maternal grandparents spoiled her with new and expensive clothes and other extravagant presents. When Roosevelt became president and the family moved to the White House, Alice was seventeen and soon became a favorite of the press and the Washington social scene. Alice had her social debut party at the White House in January 1902, and close to six hundred people attended.

The press dubbed her Princess Alice, and she became almost as popular in the media as her father. Her free-spirited behavior was considered outrageous for the times, and reporters wrote about what she wore, whom she was with, and where she went. The name Alice became very popular among parents of baby daughters at the time, and Alice's favorite shade of blue became known as "Alice blue." Alice was known for publicly smoking, betting at racetracks, flirting with men, and carrying her pet snake to parties. For more than seventy years, Alice would remain a unique and outspoken fixture of the Washington, DC, social scene.

Alice Roosevelt's popularity led the press to dub her Princess Alice.

REFORMER IN OFFICE

When Roosevelt took office, he promised to continue McKinley's policies, but McKinley had supported big business, while Roosevelt was a reformer. Businessmen worried he would push for labor reforms, and soon enough they were proven right. In 1901 a group of rich railroad owners merged their companies to create the Northern Securities Company. This monopoly controlled all railroad transportation in the West. The wealthy railroad owners were called robber barons for their unfair practices. Roosevelt quickly saw that the Northern Securities Company violated the Sherman Anti-Trust Act, which made it illegal for one company to have widespread control over services and pricing in one industry.

Passed in 1890, the Sherman Anti-Trust Act had rarely been enforced, but that didn't concern Roosevelt. In February 1902, he filed a lawsuit against the Northern Securities Company. It was the first of many businesses he broke up under the law, earning him the nickname of trust-buster. During his presidency, Roosevelt initiated forty-four trust-busting suits.

During 1902 Roosevelt had another chance to prove his commitment to reform. In May the Anthracite Coal Strike began. Miners at that time worked ten-hour days in extremely dangerous conditions. For years they'd taken pay cuts while mine owners grew wealthy. The owners also ran company stores, which were the only places to purchase goods in mining areas—and they charged very high prices. Miners had enough of the unfair practices. They wanted improved working conditions, higher pay, and shorter workdays. They also wanted their workers' union recognized. The United Mine Workers and the Western Federation of Miners had formed in 1890 and 1893 respectively, to give miners a more powerful voice in negotiations with mine owners.

In 1902, Pennsylvania miners went on strike to protest unfair work practices.

When the mine owners refused the workers' demands, 140,000 members of both unions decided to strike. As the strike wore on, coal prices rose. Winter was coming, and Americans needed coal for heat. Roosevelt took an unprecedented step for a US president and became involved with the negotiations. He stood up for the miners and even made plans for the US Army to take control of the mines if a settlement couldn't be reached. In the end, the owners were not forced to recognize the miners' unions, but the miners received a 10 percent wage increase and their workday was reduced from ten to nine hours. Roosevelt called the result a Square Deal, as all parties involved had been treated fairly.

HIGHER GOALS

Throughout his first term, Roosevelt was a powerful president. He used his position to make reforms, promote conservation of the environment, demand civil rights, and fairly negotiate deals. However, he wasn't satisfied with having inherited the presidency through the death of McKinley. He wanted Americans to elect him to be their president.

CHILDREN IN THE WHITE HOUSE

Roosevelt's children—Alice, Theodore, Kermit, Edith, Archibald, and Quentin—made the White House a playful place. The public loved hearing how the children took their pony into the White House elevator, scared a visitor with a 4-foot (1.2-meter) snake, and tossed water balloons on guards' heads. The younger children loved the large rooms in the White House. They were perfect for stilt walking and roller-skating.

The Roosevelt family in 1903: (from left) Edith, Roosevelt, Theodore Jr., Archibald, Alice, Kermit, wife Edith, and Quentin.

To make that happen, Roosevelt took calculated steps. In 1903 he showed less public support of labor over big business. He had to show a more moderate side to his politics and appear less divisive if he hoped to gain the Republican nomination for president. He also tried to win over the general public. He toured the country for thirty days and held press conferences. He even issued an executive order, a rarely issued presidential order with the force of law, to provide veterans aged sixty-two and older with pensions, making age a legal disability. This helped gain the support of Roosevelt's veteran constituents.

Once he was nominated, Roosevelt chose Senator Charles W. Fairbanks as his running mate. Fairbanks's strengths complemented Roosevelt's. Fairbanks was a more conservative politician with friends in the railroad industry.

THE TEDDY BEAR

The teddy bear was created as a toy in 1903 and named after Roosevelt. Some say the idea developed when Roosevelt refused to kill a small black bear while hunting. Dogs had cornered the bear, and his aides had tied it to a tree for Roosevelt to shoot if he so chose. But Roosevelt thought shooting the bear would be poor sportsmanship, since the bear had no chance. The *Washington Post* printed a cartoon about the event. Then toymakers took over, marketing the stuffed animal as a teddy bear, giving it the common nickname of Teddy for Theodore.

Roosevelt selected Senator Charles W. Fairbanks (right) as his running mate for the 1904 election.

Roosevelt needn't have worried about the election. He was extremely popular with the public. In 1904 he won the presidential election in a landslide. His relief was evident in a statement he made afterward: "I am no longer a political accident."

He would have four more years in office. During those years, Roosevelt planned to push his agenda to reform the nation, establish the United States as a global leader, and elevate the presidential role to a more powerful position.

Roosevelt looked forward to continued presidential service, but he promised immediately after the election that he would not run for a third term (at this time, presidents were not legally limited to two terms). All previous presidents had voluntarily limited their service as president to a maximum of two terms. He felt it was right for the country to continue the tradition.

CHAPTER THREE

ROOSEVELT THE REGULATOR

Early on in the first term of his presidency, Roosevelt showed the country he believed it was the government's responsibility to step in and take action, even in situations where government involvement was unprecedented. He was never one to simply watch from the sidelines. He said the following in a 1910 speech entitled Citizenship in a Republic:

It is not the critic who counts; not the man who points out how the strong man stumbles, or where the doer of deeds could have done them better. The credit belongs to the man who is actually in the arena, whose face is marred by dust and sweat and blood; who strives valiantly; who errs, who comes short again and again, because there is no effort without error and shortcoming; but who does actually strive to do the deeds; who knows great enthusiasms, the great devotions; who spends himself in a worthy cause; who at the best knows in the end the triumph of high achievement, and who at the worst, if he fails, at least fails while daring greatly, so that his place shall never be with those cold and timid souls who neither know victory nor defeat.

Roosevelt had a powerful speaking style. He gave thousands of speeches during his political career.

As US industry grew, Roosevelt began regulating big businesses. The country's economic disparity was growing as big businesses gained more and more power while an unskilled labor force also grew. Wealthy business owners also had the power to influence political decisions.

As president, Roosevelt saw that these conditions created societal problems in the United States. He believed if they weren't addressed, the problems might lead to rebellion and even a change in the US political structure. Roosevelt wanted to regulate big businesses to limit their power in order to protect the welfare of US society.

THE GILDED AGE TO PROGRESSIVE ERA

When Roosevelt took office as president, the Gilded Age (1870s to 1890s) in the United States had just ended. It was a period of extreme wealth for some Americans and devastating poverty for others. Industry rose and produced great wealth for business owners, such as John D. Rockefeller and Andrew Carnegie. Political corruption was also rampant. Production costs, including pay for laborers, dropped, while profit margins increased.

The rich threw extravagant parties in New York City to display their new wealth, but the majority of Americans did not fare well. Of the country's twelve million families, close to eleven million earned less than $1,200 per year, and an individual's average annual income was $380. Many urban dwellers lived in tenements with horrific living conditions. This created unrest among the working class, and it was a situation ripe for revolution against the wealthy class and government.

A mother and her children work in their New York City tenement apartment in 1911. With all family members working, this family was able to earn $6 a week, or $312 in a year.

TENEMENT SLUMS

Tenements were large apartment buildings that primarily housed poor immigrants in major cities. The buildings were poorly constructed and had very few amenities. As cities grew more crowded, tenement buildings became more crowded too. Large families of ten or twelve people often occupied small spaces, and they sometimes took in boarders to help pay the rent. The buildings weren't designed to offer light and proper ventilation to renters. Apartments often did not have a water supply or bathrooms. The overcrowding caused many sanitation problems and disease spread quickly in tenement neighborhoods. Poor maintenance caused tenements to rapidly degrade as well.

New government laws improved tenements with increased ventilation, fireproofing features, minimum room sizes, and improved toilet facilities. But many tenements proved unfit for habitation and were eventually torn down in the 1930s.

As president, Roosevelt led the United States' new Progressive Era, which began in 1901. Progressives sought reforms, including a stronger role for the government in controlling businesses and protecting the rights of workers, women, African Americans, and consumers. There were no government controls on how companies treated workers, and workers did not have a legal right to form unions for their protection. If they didn't do what their bosses demanded, no matter how unfair or unsafe, they could be fired. Companies could force people to work sixty to seventy hours per week.

They hired children to perform dangerous jobs. Wages were extremely low. Bosses could physically and verbally abuse workers, who had no power to fight back without risking their jobs. If they were fired unfairly, they had no legal rights to unemployment pay.

As president, Roosevelt had the power to take action. He knew he could address issues associated with working and living conditions and the pricing of goods sold to the general public. He used his office to establish new regulations and laws whenever he could.

Roosevelt had shocked the country when he filed suit to break up the Northern Securities Company under the Sherman Anti-Trust Act. He surprised Americans again when he stepped

Roosevelt sent a commission of officials to investigate complaints made by coal miners during the Anthracite Coal Strike.

in to help negotiate an end the Anthracite Coal Strike, convincing mine owners and labor representatives to allow a commission to settle their differences.

The phrase "Square Deal" came to have a larger meaning in his presidency. Roosevelt used it to describe his domestic program for the country. Roosevelt's goal was to help build a society where all citizens were treated fairly. He believed everyone should have access to economic opportunities, be able to earn a good living, and succeed. In the past, many government policies had favored the wealthy and big business owners. Roosevelt decided to change that.

REGULATING RAILROADS

In his first term, Roosevelt began addressing these concerns with specific measures. One segment of society he was determined to regulate was the railroad industry. Too much power allowed railroads to hike rates beyond what passengers and shipping companies found reasonable. Railroads unfairly favored large shipping companies by offering reduced rates for them, but not for smaller companies. This punished smaller shipping companies.

The issue of rebates was also a problem within the railroad industry. Large shipping companies had the power to demand rebates from railroad companies. These rebates were secret refunds of money to the shipping companies from the railroads. The shipping companies paid higher prices up front and then received money back from the railroad companies. This lowered actual costs for the large shipping companies, but other companies still had to pay the higher prices and did not receive rebates. If the large shippers' demands weren't met, they might threaten to take their business to other railroad companies. It kept the railroad companies hostage to the demands of large shippers.

Roosevelt approved regulations that standardized rates for railroad services.

Roosevelt's first attempt to regulate railroad companies resulted in the Elkins Act in 1903. The Elkins Act outlawed rebates, which satisfied railroad companies and also helped farmers and other smaller shippers who didn't have the power to make such demands. The act ensured standard rates for railroad services, so certain companies couldn't receive special rates. The Interstate Commerce Commission (ICC) set the rates, and the Elkins Act upheld them. The government created the ICC in 1887 to oversee railroads and set guidelines for how they conducted business.

The Elkins Act didn't control the railroad industry to the extent Roosevelt intended, however. The federal government and the ICC needed more power over railroad companies to make sure rates remained affordable for passengers and shippers. So in 1906, Roosevelt signed the Hepburn Act. This law further empowered the ICC so it could ensure railroad companies followed the law.

FOOD SAFETY STANDARDS

Through regulation, Roosevelt helped protect the public in other ways as well. In 1906 journalist Upton Sinclair published the novel *The Jungle*, which exposed unsanitary conditions in the meatpacking industry. Americans who read the book realized that the meat they purchased was often rotten and diseased. Sinclair described sausages made of rotten ham, rat droppings, and whole poisoned rats. He told how workers had no sinks or soap to clean their hands, even after using the bathroom. Readers were disgusted and outraged.

While the book was a work of fiction that mainly focused on the experiences of an immigrant family, the details about the meatpacking industry were true. Sinclair based them on his own experiences working in a meatpacking factory.

Men and boys stuff sausage skins in a Chicago meatpacking factory in 1893. Upton Sinclair described the unsanitary conditions of the meatpacking industry in his 1906 novel The Jungle.

THE JUNGLE

Upton Sinclair joined the Socialist Party in 1903 and began writing for a Socialist magazine. He witnessed the Chicago meatpacking strike in 1904 as meat-packers fought for better wages and working conditions. Instead of granting these requests, the meatpacking companies brought in replacement workers as the strikers fell into poverty.

In response, Sinclair decided to investigate and write about the working conditions of the meatpacking plants and strike in Chicago. He witnessed the conditions firsthand and also interviewed workers and their families, lawyers, doctors, and social workers. An installment of *The Jungle* was first published in 1905 and then it was released as a novel in 1906. It became an international best seller and alerted the public to the way in which their food was being processed.

While *The Jungle* led to changes that protected consumers, Sinclair was disappointed that it didn't also lead to protection for laborers. He told the media, "I aimed at the public's heart, and by accident I hit it in the stomach."

Sinclair wrote The Jungle in an effort to improve conditions for laborers.

Roosevelt didn't take Sinclair seriously at first. During a speech in 1906, he used the term *muckraker*. He was referring to whistle-blowing journalists, such as Sinclair, who "raked muck," or dug up dirt on industries and stirred up trouble for the public. Though Roosevelt had meant to insult Sinclair, as Roosevelt did not appreciate the author's accusation that government inspectors were not performing their duties, Sinclair embraced the term as one that fit his mission to expose ugly truths.

However, Roosevelt didn't dismiss Sinclair's claims. He ordered a Department of Agriculture investigation of the meat inspection system. The investigators found that what Sinclair had written was true. Conditions were as bad as he'd described or worse. They even saw workers accidentally drop a pig carcass into a toilet, then pull it out for packing without cleaning it.

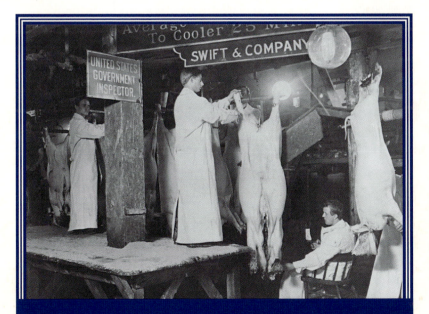

Government inspectors examine hog carcasses at a Chicago meatpacking facility in the early 1900s.

The meatpacking industry wasn't the only big business taking advantage of workers and consumers. The government did not regulate food or drugs sold to the public. Drug companies made cough, cold, and pain medicines with addictive narcotics such as heroin, morphine, and cocaine. Food companies colored children's candy with toxic materials and other foods with coal tar, a poisonous liquid by-product of coal.

Once Roosevelt had his investigators' report, the government took action. Under Roosevelt's leadership, Congress passed the Pure Food and Drug Act and the Federal Meat Inspection Act, which became law on June 30, 1906. These laws set standards for the meatpacking, food, and drug industries. The Meat Inspection Act aimed to ensure that food was safe to eat. It mandated that the Department of Agriculture inspect meat before and after processing, which had to be done in sanitary conditions. The Pure Food and Drug Act required manufacturers to label food

DUBIOUS DRUGS

Before Roosevelt's time, drug companies could make great profits promising impossible cures for different diseases. Medicines such as antibiotics hadn't yet been developed, and people could die from something as small as a scratch that became infected. False claims lured in customers who were willing and eager to try anything. The label on William Radam's Microbe Killer read, "Cures all diseases." Ads for Dr. Sibley's Solar Tincture even claimed it would "restore life in the event of sudden death."

and drugs with a complete and accurate list of their ingredients and the Bureau of Chemistry in the Department of Agriculture enforced the law.

Though Roosevelt made a reputation for himself as a regulator, he wasn't an enemy of big business in the United States. He believed corporations had an important place in the country's economy. He said the following in his State of the Union address in 1902:

> *Our aim is not to do away with corporations; on the contrary, these big aggregations are an inevitable development of modern industrialism, and the effort to destroy them would be futile unless accomplished in ways that would work the utmost mischief to the entire body politic. We can do nothing of good in the way of regulating and supervising these corporations until we fix clearly in our minds that we are not attacking the corporations, but endeavoring to do away with any evil in them. We are not hostile to them; we are merely determined that they shall be so handled as to subserve the public good. We draw the line against misconduct, not against wealth.*

Roosevelt also knew that if he committed to ideas that were too radical—such as abolishing corporations—he would become an unpopular president. When he came into office, Roosevelt needed to lead where McKinley left off. When he ran for a second term, he needed conservative Republicans, who supported big business, in his corner.

CHAPTER FOUR

FOREIGN POLICY

When Roosevelt took office, he had big dreams for his country's position in the world. After the Spanish-American War, the nation had acquired land overseas for the first time. The United States had emerged victoriously as a world power with overseas outposts and now had international responsibilities in global affairs. Roosevelt saw that a delicate balance of international relationships maintained peace. Yet he wanted to spread US influence around the globe, become the dominant power in the Pacific, and become actively involved in the stability of Caribbean countries.

Like Roosevelt's domestic policy, his foreign policy had a colorful description: "Speak softly and carry a big stick." Roosevelt wanted the United States to aim for peace using arbitration, or formal meetings and negotiations, to settle differences between countries. This attitude was described by the "speak softly" part of his slogan. He was also ready to used armed force if necessary, which was the "big stick" part of the phrase.

Roosevelt began building the country's military, specifically the US Navy. He convinced Congress to approve funding to add battleships and sailors until the US Navy became one of the world's largest. The white battleships earned the navy's nickname of the Great White Fleet.

In 1904 Roosevelt also demonstrated an aggressive attitude toward South America and the Caribbean. He was concerned that European countries might invade the South American country of Venezuela to demand payment of debts owed to them, and he wanted to limit European power in the Western Hemisphere. Roosevelt wanted to intervene against the Europeans, provided the United States maintained control of the area. To justify US involvement, Roosevelt extended US powers stated in the Monroe Doctrine of 1823 with the Roosevelt Corollary in 1904 and 1905.

Roosevelt used the phrase "speak softly and carry a big stick" to describe his foreign policy. Political cartoons of the early 1900s show Roosevelt as the world's policeman carrying a large baton to keep other countries in line.

The Monroe Doctrine had become US foreign policy under President James Monroe (1817–1825). At that time, many colonies in South America were gaining their independence from European powers. The doctrine warned powerful European countries to not interfere in the Western Hemisphere, including North and South America, Central America, and the Caribbean. The US government would not tolerate European countries setting up new colonies or interfering with independent governments. In return, the United States would not interfere in European affairs in the Eastern Hemisphere.

The Monroe Doctrine was a statement of principle. It was not a law or diplomatic tool. The Roosevelt Corollary was a justification

THE PHILIPPINES

After the Spanish-American War, the Philippine-American War (1899–1902) broke out. The Philippines fought for independence from outside rule, but the United States won the war and gained control. McKinley appointed William Howard Taft the civilian governor of the Philippines in 1901. The US military was brutally fighting against a Filipino rebellion, and the US press attacked the government about the United States' conduct there. While there, Taft drafted a constitution for the country, established laws and a judicial system, and formed a new government, with the civilian governor in a central role. Later, in 1904, Roosevelt appointed Taft to be the secretary of war. Taft went on to become the twenty-seventh president of the United States in 1909.

The United States sent troops into Cuba, Nicaragua, Haiti, and the Dominican Republic as part of the Roosevelt Corollary policy.

for international policing action. It stated that the United States would get involved if necessary to prevent European invasion. It set up the United States to act as a global policing power to prevent unrest in Latin American and Caribbean countries.

The US government sent troops into Cuba in 1906, Nicaragua in 1907, and Haiti and the Dominican Republic in 1914. The policy was fairly popular among Americans, who saw its use as a demonstration of the United States' rising world power. In Latin American countries, a US presence was at first welcomed but was later met with mistrust as countries wondered what purpose these troops truly served.

THE GREAT WHITE FLEET

Roosevelt wanted the world to know of the United States' naval strength. He also wanted to test his new battleships for battle readiness while gaining support from the public for the naval shipbuilding program. In 1907 the Great White Fleet began touring the globe. Sixteen battleships and fourteen thousand sailors made the trip. Crowds in South American ports cheered for and welcomed the fleet. Japanese children sang "The Star-Spangled Banner" and waved US flags as the ships came to their country. And while some worried that the fleet might be attacked and destroyed while on tour, nothing happened. The fleet traveled for fourteen months and returned to Virginia in February 1909.

The Great White Fleet set sail on their goodwill mission around the world on December 16, 1907.

PEACEMAKING PRESIDENT

Some believed Roosevelt's foreign policy slogan indicated he was aggressive toward foreign countries. He also carried this reputation from before his presidency, due to his eagerness to fight in the Spanish-American War. But as president, Roosevelt proved himself to be a world peacemaker.

In 1902 Roosevelt became the first world leader to use the international Permanent Court of Arbitration at The Hague, a city in the Netherlands. Founded in 1899 at the First Hague Peace Conference by twenty-six governments, it hadn't yet been used to help negotiate international disputes. Roosevelt submitted a dispute between the United States and Mexico to the court for its resolution. The two countries could not agree on whether Mexico was still obligated to fund the Pious Fund of the Californias, a government-managed fund used by religious missions in the area of California. Upper California had become part of the United States in 1848 and Mexico refused to pay the fund to church officials there. The two governments could not come to an agreement on whether the Mexican government should continue to administer the fund to church officials. The Permanent Court of Arbitration ruled in favor of the United States and required Mexico to pay the fund.

Roosevelt also arbitrated a dispute between France and Germany over control of Morocco. This crisis could have escalated into war. He worked with both sides and persuaded them to attend a conference to settle their dispute. The Algeciras Conference began on January 16, 1906. Talks hit a standstill though and almost failed, but Roosevelt presented a compromise that settled their dispute and averted war.

Another foreign issue soon involved Roosevelt. When Japan attacked Russia, it began the Russo-Japanese War (1904–1905). Japan wanted to gain control over China and Korea and stop Russia from doing so. In just one battle, Russia lost sixty thousand

soldiers and Japan lost forty-one thousand. In 1905 both countries were ready to end the war and Roosevelt stepped forward to offer help. Leaders from Russia and Japan met with him in Portsmouth, New Hampshire. Within a few weeks, they negotiated peace between the countries. Russia, torn by unrest at home, agreed to leave China and accept Japanese control of Korea.

In 1906 Roosevelt received the Nobel Peace Prize for his role in ending the war. He was the first president and the first American to win the award. Roosevelt donated his award money to fund a permanent industrial peace committee, although this did not materialize. He was unable to accept the award in person and, instead, delivered his acceptance speech by telegram. In it he explained that "in modern life it is as important to work for the cause of just and righteous peace in the industrial world as in the world of nations."

Roosevelt (center) introduces Russian and Japanese delegates during the Portsmouth Peace Conference in 1905. Roosevelt was awarded the Nobel Peace Prize for his work in negotiating the peace treaty.

RUSSO-JAPANESE NEGOTIATIONS

Most Americans sided with Japan during the Russo-Japanese War, but Roosevelt tried to be fair to both countries when negotiating peace between them. Both gained and lost in the Treaty of Portsmouth. Japan won control of Korea and the southern parts of Manchuria and Sakhalin Island. Russia had to give up part of Sakhalin Island, but the country was not obligated to pay Japan's war expenses. After the treaty was signed, riots broke out, as many were unhappy with the terms. Over time, however, relations between Japan and Russia improved.

THE PANAMA CANAL

While Roosevelt's foreign policy did not focus solely on waging war, he didn't hesitate to use military force if he thought it would advance the strength and influence of the United States. He believed that the United States should have a more prominent place in the global economy. This was hampered by the months-long journey ships had to make to transport goods between the Atlantic Ocean and Pacific Ocean. By cutting a canal through Panama, a narrow country in Central America, the journey could be made faster and cheaper than before. Political leaders and business owners in the United States and Europe had been pushing for it for years. Without a canal, ships traveling between New York City and San Francisco, California, had to take a perilous 12,000-mile (19,300-km) trip around Cape Horn in South America. The canal would allow ships to sail through Central America instead.

The French had attempted to build a canal in 1881. Millions of dollars and thousands of deaths later, they gave up. While

Roosevelt couldn't take credit for the idea, he could try again to make it a reality. In 1901 he started working to gain support for the Panama Canal. Roosevelt negotiated extensively for its construction with Colombia, the country that controlled Panama. When Colombia did not agree to the terms, Roosevelt led the United States in support of Panama's revolution for independence from Colombia. A short battle ended with Colombia's defeat and the formation of the nation of Panama in 1903. This cleared the way for the canal's construction.

In 1906, two years after the construction of the canal began, Roosevelt went to Panama to observe the work. He became the first president in US history to travel outside the country while in office. After ten years of construction, the canal was finished

Roosevelt (center) observes the progress of the Panama Canal during his 1906 visit to the site.

DISEASE ON THE CANAL

Workers on the Panama Canal risked their health and their lives. The area was a dense jungle, filled with poisonous snakes and disease-carrying insects. The rainy season between May and November coated the wet workers in mud. They had poor living and sanitary conditions, being housed in dilapidated barracks. Many became ill with yellow fever, which was often fatal, and malaria spread as well. Both diseases caused debilitating symptoms including fevers, fatigue, nausea, and vomiting. In 1906 alone, approximately 80 percent of the workers contracted malaria.

There wasn't much doctors could do for laborers who contracted yellow fever and malaria. Some prescribed whiskey or rubbed kerosene and oil on their patients' skin. Some gave them quinine, a liquid made from tree bark that reduced fever but also caused deafness.

Chief Medical Officer William Gorgas believed the diseases spread easily and quickly by mosquitoes in Panama's humid climate. In 1905 Roosevelt agreed to fund Gorgas's $1 million plan to rid the area of mosquitoes. It took time, but by 1906, yellow fever was no longer a threat, and by 1910, the malaria death rate was less than 1 percent.

in 1914. It had been built by almost forty-five thousand workers and had cost $375 million. The passageway cut travel time for ships considerably. The trip from San Francisco to New York City was reduced by more than 8,000 miles (12,900 km). Travel time was cut in half for vessels from sixty to thirty days. The canal's completion cemented the United States' position of power in the global economy.

★ CHAPTER FIVE ★

CIVIL RIGHTS

Many of Roosevelt's domestic policies and decisions focused on social justice. As president he wanted to ensure a square deal for all Americans. On the issue of civil rights, however, he didn't always take a strong stance. Throughout his time in office, Roosevelt went back and forth with his support for African Americans and other racial minorities.

In one of his first acts as president, Roosevelt demonstrated his belief that African Americans deserved fair and equal treatment. Soon after taking office in 1901, Roosevelt invited Booker T. Washington, the African American president of the Tuskegee Institute, to dine with him at the White House. Slavery had been abolished only thirty-six years earlier in 1865. The practice was still legal in the United States when Roosevelt was a child. In fact, Booker T. Washington had been born a slave.

Before 1901 other US presidents had met with African American leaders at the White House. But they had never invited an African American leader to share a meal there. It wasn't a planned invitation from Roosevelt—he made the decision impulsively. Then, knowing it would stir up controversy, he

It created controversy throughout the country when Booker T. Washington (left) dined with Roosevelt at the White House in 1901, as depicted in this illustration created years after the event.

immediately questioned the idea. His hesitation made him feel ashamed, and because of that, he went through with it.

At the time, the United States had laws that segregated African Americans and white Americans in both public and private life. The dinner invitation outraged many southerners, who considered African Americans inferior to whites. Many southerners were offended by more than the thought of an African American man eating with the president. At that time in history, such an invitation was symbolic. It meant that Roosevelt considered Washington a social equal.

They were further scandalized to learn that when Washington dined at the White House, female members of the First Family were also at the table. Roosevelt's wife Edith attended the dinner, as did his daughter Alice. Socializing between men and women of different races was unacceptable for many at the time. It flouted the principles of segregation in every way.

Although slavery had been abolished by the time Roosevelt became president, many African Americans were subjected to segregation and continued financial hardship and racial prejudice.

When the story of the dinner hit the newspapers, southern politicians spoke out angrily against Roosevelt. They felt he had put his personal views about racial equality into a public forum, where they didn't belong. The politicians promised they wouldn't go along with Roosevelt's agenda. A story in the *Memphis Scimitar* stated that the dinner was the greatest "outrage which has ever been perpetrated by any citizen of the United States."

The *Richmond Times* reported: "It means that the president is willing that Negroes shall mingle freely with whites in the social circle—that white women may receive attentions from negro men; it means that there is no racial reason in his opinion why whites and blacks may not marry and intermarry, why the Anglo-Saxon may not mix negro blood with his blood."

Roosevelt stood his ground publicly. He declared he would rather lose his political friends than his self-respect. Still, he didn't extend another dinner invitation to Washington or any other African American while in office.

EXPANDING THE CHINESE EXCLUSION ACT

Roosevelt soon faced another major decision regarding civil rights in the United States. In 1902 he expanded the Chinese Exclusion Act of 1882. The law singled out Chinese laborers, preventing them from immigrating to the United States for a period of ten years. They were also not eligible to become US citizens.

This blatantly discriminatory act had been the first law in US history to restrict immigration based upon ethnicity. Over time the US government expanded it in several ways. In 1888 Congress passed the Scott Act. This law prevented Chinese people who were living legally in the United States from visiting China and then returning to the United States. If they left, they would never be allowed back in. In 1892 the Geary Act extended the Chinese Exclusion Act for another ten years.

Chinese men and boys gather in Chinatown in San Francisco, California, in 1901. Chinese immigrants were barred from entering the United States beginning in 1882.

CHINESE DISCRIMINATION

When Chinese laborers immigrated to the United States in the 1850s, they worked in gold mines, on farms, and in factories. They were a huge labor force in building the country's first transcontinental railroad. The Central Pacific Railroad hired more than twelve thousand Chinese workers. Yet their contributions to the United States made them targets for discrimination and, eventually, retribution.

US workers resented Chinese laborers, who worked for lower wages. Racist sentiments took hold. White Americans embraced the idea that Chinese neighborhoods were corrupt and Chinese people were immoral. They believed keeping Chinese immigrants out of the United States would be a good solution to this perceived problem.

The California state government responded by passing laws that discriminated against Chinese people by making it difficult for them to open businesses and stay in the United States. Over time, the federal government worked to limit Chinese immigration, eventually passing the Chinese Exclusion Act.

Thousands of Chinese immigrants worked on western railroad projects.

Roosevelt stated his opinion on the matter in his first message to Congress on December 3, 1901. "The Chinese Exclusion Act should be re-enacted," he said, "for the American wage-earner must be protected against cheap labor. The Chinese and illiterate foreigners should be debarred." The president chose to expand the law in 1902 so that Chinese immigrants from Hawaii and the Philippines were also kept out of the United States. Not long after, the Chinese Exclusion Act was extended again. This time, there was no expiration date on the law.

In 1905 China responded by boycotting US goods. The protest didn't last long, however, because merchants dealing in US goods did not want to continue. The Chinese government then turned against the boycott too. Discriminatory laws in the United States kept Chinese immigrants from becoming US citizens and entering the country until 1943, when the ban was lifted.

DEFENDING MINNIE COX

The year after he expanded the Chinese Exclusion Act, Roosevelt championed the cause of Minnie Cox, the African American postmistress in charge of the post office in Indianola, Mississippi.

President Benjamin Harrison had appointed Cox to her federal position in 1891. It was a high-paying job in her community, and Cox was a dedicated worker. She willingly used her personal money to install a telephone in the post office. She also paid the late rent on post office boxes, so local residents wouldn't be inconvenienced.

Over time, however, resentment about her appointment grew among some white citizens in her community. They wanted Cox removed from the position, so it would be available for a white worker. Her term wasn't over until 1904, though, and she refused to step down early.

The situation grew volatile. The editor of the local newspaper the *Greenwood Commonwealth*, who wanted the job, publicly spoke out against Cox. When white residents threatened her with violence, Cox felt she had no choice but to resign the position in January 1903.

Roosevelt refused to accept her resignation. He ordered the prosecution of those who'd threatened Cox. And instead of appointing someone else to the position, he closed the Indianola post office. His decisive action indicated he would not tolerate racist pressure on the federal government. He even made sure Cox was paid for the year the office was closed.

Southern politicians objected to Roosevelt's actions. They accused the president of trying to win over African American voters and argued that he should have supported the white citizens in Indianola. When the post office reopened, Roosevelt appointed William Martin, a white man recommended by Cox, to the postmaster position. Cox went on to open a bank with her husband.

THE BROWNSVILLE AFFAIR

Two years after the post office incident, Roosevelt appeared to reverse his position toward African Americans. In 1906 some white residents of Brownsville, Texas, accused a group of African American soldiers of shooting a white bartender and injuring a police officer. The soldiers were from nearby Fort Brown and had white commanders who vouched for their whereabouts. The commanders told officials the soldiers were in the barracks when the shooting took place.

White townspeople told a different story. They claimed to have witnessed the shooting, and some even claimed to have shells from the soldiers' guns. Investigators believed the shells were probably planted. Still, the investigators took the white community's word over that of the African American soldiers. As the situation developed, it became known as the Brownsville Affair.

AFRICAN AMERICAN VOTING RIGHTS

The US government granted African American men the right to vote under the Fifteenth Amendment to the US Constitution in 1870. But in practice, African Americans were often denied this right. Many southern states required literacy tests that uneducated people could not pass. They enforced unfair poll taxes that many could not pay. White supremacist groups such as the Ku Klux Klan believed that white people were racially superior to African Americans, and they used physical threats and violence to stop African Americans from voting.

As president, Roosevelt did not address this situation. He believed that some African American individuals, such as Washington, were equals to white individuals. But as a whole, he felt African Americans were inferior to white citizens. Roosevelt wrote in the *North American Review* in 1895 that "a perfectly stupid race can never rise to a very high plane; the negro, for instance, has been kept down as much by lack of intellectual development as by anything else."

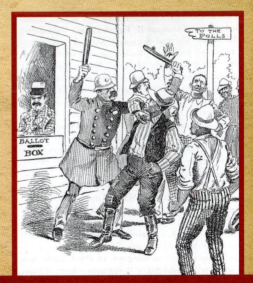

An 1899 illustration depicts African Americans being denied their vote.

African Americans were able to enlist in segregated regiments of the US Army beginning in the 1860s.

Military leaders ordered the African American soldiers to either confess or turn in the culprits. The soldiers said they didn't know who had committed the crime and refused to offer names of possible killers. No court hearing was held, and prosecutors had no solid evidence to convict the soldiers. Army investigators felt the soldiers weren't cooperating. Roosevelt waited to act until after African American voters had elected Republican candidates in the November elections. Then, instead of giving the soldiers a chance to stand trial, he ordered the army to dishonorably discharge the soldiers. The army discharged 167 African American soldiers. Some were close to earning their pensions after decades of service. With dishonorable discharges, they lost all the benefits they had earned.

WOMEN'S SUFFRAGE

In 1898 Roosevelt expressed his lack of interest in the issue of women's voting rights to Susan B. Anthony, a leader of the women's suffrage movement. In 1904 Roosevelt and his wife hosted four hundred women's suffrage leaders at the White House. But the president did not officially support the movement. Another leader in the movement, Harriet Burton Laidlaw, spoke to him about women's right to vote in 1907. He still would not give his support.

Four years after his presidency ended, however, in 1913 Roosevelt changed his stance on women's suffrage. He gave the issue his full support. He said, "Conservative friends tell me that woman's duty is the home. Certainly. So is man's. The duty of a woman to the home isn't any more than the man's. If any married man doesn't know that the woman pulls a little more than her share in the home he needs education . . . The average woman needs fifteen minutes to vote, and I want to point out to the alarmist that she will have left 364 days, twenty-three hours and forty-five minutes." Women won the right to vote in 1919, with the Nineteenth Amendment to the US Constitution.

Harriet Burton Laidlaw (right) campaigned for women's right to vote.

White and African American citizens alike disagreed with the decision. Booker T. Washington pleaded with Roosevelt to reconsider, but the president stood firm. He said, "You cannot have any information to give me privately to which I could pay heed, my dear Mr. Washington, because the information on which I act is that which came out of the investigation itself."

LONG-TERM APPROACH

Though Roosevelt wanted to promote fairness and equality throughout the nation, he did not always make choices that supported civil rights. In cases such as the Brownsville Affair and the Chinese Exclusion Act, his decisions followed prevailing racist attitudes. Some believed he was soft on civil rights.

Booker T. Washington (center) watches Roosevelt deliver a speech in Tuskegee, Alabama, on October 24, 1905.

Still, Roosevelt took small steps to move the country toward more tolerance and social justice. His support of certain African American individuals, such as Washington and Cox, helped push civil rights slowly forward. In 1905 Roosevelt made a speech to the New York City Republican Club, encouraging white Americans to be more accepting of other races. Unwilling to make major changes, he advocated for a gradual, long-term approach to racial equality.

★ CHAPTER SIX ★

CONSERVATION

When Roosevelt became president, he brought to the office his perspective as a lifelong naturalist. His interest in wildlife and the environment went back much farther than his political career. Roosevelt had enjoyed the natural world as a child. His concern about protecting the United States' natural resources deepened and became a priority of his presidency. He wanted to prevent natural resources from being squandered and ruined by individuals and businesses. Roosevelt wanted to more efficiently use natural resources, ensuring their lasting use by future generations. In Roosevelt's first message to Congress, he said forest reserves should be "set apart forever, for the use and benefit of our people as a whole and not sacrificed to the shortsighted greed of a few."

Increasing the number of national parks was of great concern to the president. The first in the country was Yellowstone National Park, which was established in 1872. While it had been declared a national park, no enforcing laws against its development were passed. Tourism was a big threat. Promoters built resorts on the land, cut down trees, and even wanted to build a railroad through Yellowstone for sightseers. It was destroying Yellowstone and its wildlife. The Boone & Crockett Club, which Roosevelt helped found, campaigned against its destruction, and Congress passed the Park Protection Act in 1894 to save Yellowstone from further destruction.

Loggers, miners, and other commercial interests continued to threaten other national parks and natural resources. No central governmental organization existed to manage them. As a result, the parks' resources were exploited. As settlers continued moving west, displacing American Indian tribes and repurposing the land for agriculture, the future of many of the country's natural resources seemed grim. Roosevelt had witnessed how some big-game species, such as the once great bison herds, were on the verge of extinction from overhunting. Smaller animals and birds were threatened by overgrazing of the country's grasslands.

Roosevelt explores Yellowstone National Park in April 1903.

NATIONAL PARKS AND RESERVES

As soon as he became president, Roosevelt began signing legislation to establish five new national parks, in Colorado, North Dakota, Oklahoma, Oregon, and South Dakota. This doubled the existing number of national parks in the United States. The federal government designated these areas to be protected from development and preserved for public enjoyment. In all, Roosevelt preserved more than 150 million acres (61 million hectares) of land.

In 1903 he established Pelican Island National Wildlife Refuge in Florida. It was the country's first federal bird reservation, an area where wild birds are protected from hunters and their habitats are protected from destruction. Roosevelt went on to establish fifty more bird reservations while in office. And in 1905, he established Wichita Forest and Game Preserve in Oklahoma.

Roosevelt established five national parks between 1902 and 1906.

Pelican Island National Wildlife Refuge was created to protect Florida's bird habitats. It was the first federal bird reservation in the country.

It was the country's first protected area for big game, including bison, elk, deer, and other animals.

That year Roosevelt established the US Forest Service, which allowed the government more control over national forests. He appointed Gifford Pinchot to head the organization. Together, Roosevelt and Pinchot developed a vision for both conserving and using the country's forests. Logging and grazing could continue as needed to support the growing nation. However, the government would oversee those uses so the forests would be sustainable. During his presidency, Roosevelt set aside 150 national forests and protected them from development and destruction.

Not everyone welcomed Roosevelt's conservation efforts. Some objected to the inclusion of non-forest land within forest reserves. Roosevelt addressed this objection by signing the Forest Homestead Act in 1906. The new law allowed people to settle on plots of land suited for agriculture in forest reserves.

AMERICAN INDIAN LANDS

The creation of national parks and monuments often completely disregarded the interests and historical significance of the sites to American Indian tribes. American Indians had occupied Yellowstone for more than ten thousand years. Devils Tower, a geologic rock formation in Wyoming, was long used as a center of prayer for several American Indian tribes. The Miwok tribe called the Yosemite area home for more than four thousand years before European newcomers arrived.

As national parks were created, thousands of American Indian people were displaced, evicted from their tribal homes of centuries. In Roosevelt's opinion, American Indians were "hopelessly incompetent to better themselves or to utilize [the United States] to advantage without white leadership and direction." Like many whites of the time, Roosevelt believed white interests were more important than those of American Indian tribes.

Devils Tower is a sacred site for many American Indian tribes.

USING RESOURCES

Roosevelt wanted to do more than set aside natural resources for future use. He also wanted natural resources to benefit people living in arid lands. Having been a rancher in the Dakota Territory as a young man, Roosevelt knew how westerners suffered from lack of water. In a 1901 speech, he said, "The reclamation of the unsettled arid public lands presents a different problem. Here it is not enough to regulate the flow of streams. The object of the Government is to dispose of the land to settlers who will build homes upon it. To accomplish this object water must be brought within their reach."

In 1902 Roosevelt signed the Newlands Reclamation Act into law. It authorized the government to divert water to dry areas of the country so families and farmers could cultivate and live on the land. The original Newlands Reclamation Act

The Newlands Reclamation Act allowed the government to build dams, such as the Theodore Roosevelt Dam (above), to divert water to dry lands.

named sixteen states in need of water. They included Arizona, California, Colorado, Idaho, Kansas, Montana, Nebraska, Nevada, New Mexico, North Dakota, Oklahoma, Oregon, South Dakota, Utah, Washington, and Wyoming. In 1906 Texas was added to the list.

The Newlands Reclamation Act led to projects such as the Theodore Roosevelt Dam, on Arizona's Salt River. The dam diverted water so that desert land could be used for farming. The Lower Yellowstone Irrigation District was also created under the act. It provided water to areas of North Dakota and Montana. The dams built under the project made thousands of acres of land usable for residents and farmers. These engineering feats would also forever alter the environment and river ecosystems.

NATIONAL MONUMENTS

In addition to his conservation efforts, Roosevelt was concerned with preserving sites important to US history and science. In 1906 he signed the Antiquities Act into law. The new law protected specific areas from looting, destruction, and development by declaring that they had historic or scientific significance. Roosevelt used the law to establish Devils Tower as the country's first national monument. He went on to set aside seventeen more sites as scientific areas or national monuments, including the Grand Canyon in Arizona.

FURTHER EFFORTS

In May 1908, the first Conference of Governors met at the White House to discuss conservation. The following month, Roosevelt created the National Conservation Commission to inventory the country's natural resources. He wanted to better understand what natural resources were available and which resources needed protection.

NATIONAL MONUMENTS ESTABLISHED BY ROOSEVELT

1906

Devils Tower, Wyoming
El Morro, New Mexico
Montezuma Castle, Arizona
Petrified Forest, Arizona

1907

Lassen Peak, California
Cinder Cone, California
Chaco Canyon, New Mexico
Gila Cliff Dwellings, New Mexico
Tonto Cliff Dwellings, Arizona

1908

Muir Woods, California
Grand Canyon, Arizona
Pinnacles, California
Jewel Cave, South Dakota
Natural Bridges, Utah
Lewis & Clark Cavern, Montana
Tumacácori Mission, Arizona
Wheeler, Colorado

1909

Mount Olympus, Washington

Roosevelt addressed the need for conservation efforts in a speech at the conference. "We have become great in a material sense because of the lavish use of our resources, and we have just reason to be proud of our growth. But the time has come to inquire seriously what will happen when our forests are gone, when the coal, the iron, the oil, and the gas are exhausted, when the soils shall have been still further impoverished and washed into the streams, polluting the rivers, denuding the fields, and obstructing navigation," he said.

Before he left office in 1909, Roosevelt convened the North American Conservation Conference at the White House to

The North American Conservation Conference met at the White House in 1909. Delegates from Canada, Mexico, and the United States met with Roosevelt (bottom row, center) to discuss conservation efforts for the continent.

discuss principles and recommendations for future conservation efforts. One recommendation was for an international conservation conference.

Roosevelt wrote in a 1908 letter, "It is evident that natural resources are not limited by the boundary lines which separate nations, and that the need for conserving them upon this continent is as wide as the area upon which they exist."

★ CHAPTER SEVEN ★

A LASTING LEGACY

When Roosevelt's second term ended, he kept the promise he had made after the 1904 election about not running again for president. Instead, he supported his good friend William Howard Taft for the presidency. Taft had served as the civilian governor of the Philippines and US secretary of war.

After Taft won the 1908 election, Roosevelt embarked on an ambitious African safari with his son Kermit and a team. Roosevelt had always wanted to hunt big game in Africa. The trip, cosponsored by the Smithsonian Institution, lasted for eleven months. Roosevelt and his son shot or trapped thousands of animals, including twenty rhinoceroses, seventeen lions, eleven elephants, and nine giraffes. The animals were eaten or preserved and donated to today's National Museum of Natural History. The expedition also brought live animals back to the National Zoological Park, including lions, cheetahs, and gazelles.

By 1912, when Taft planned to run for a second term, Roosevelt did not support him. In fact, Roosevelt felt Taft had been disloyal to him. Roosevelt was angry that Taft had fired Gifford Pinchot, chief of the US Forest Service. Furthermore, Roosevelt did not approve of Taft's policies and felt he had not been enough of

*Roosevelt and his son Kermit traveled to Africa on a
big game hunting trip in 1909.*

a reformer while in office. With these issues weighing on him,
Roosevelt changed his mind about running for president again.

CHALLENGING TAFT

For months Roosevelt campaigned to gain public support as the
1912 Republican candidate for president. He proposed more reforms,
including laws to tax higher- and lower-income levels differently
and prevent politicians from using corporate funds for political
purposes. His ideas became known as the New Nationalism.

Beyond promoting his national agenda, Roosevelt also
attacked Taft. He criticized Taft's politics in public speeches and
even attacked Taft personally, calling the candidate a "fathead"
and a "puzzle wit." Taft fought back, but it was a painful time
for both men, and Roosevelt mourned the loss of the friendship
they'd once had.

MOUNT RUSHMORE

In 1927 four hundred men and women began work on Mount Rushmore, in the Black Hills of South Dakota. The memorial depicts the faces of four US presidents carved into a granite mountainside: George Washington, Thomas Jefferson, Abraham Lincoln, and Theodore Roosevelt. Sculptor Gutzon Borglum chose presidents who changed the country within its first 150 years. He chose Roosevelt for his work on the Panama Canal and because of his dedication to fighting big business and helping the common worker. It took close to fourteen years to finish the massive sculpture, which was completed in 1941.

Mount Rushmore is a national memorial honoring four presidents who changed the United States.

Though the primary elections proved Roosevelt was popular with the people, Taft won the Republican nomination. Taft supporters dominated the Republican National Committee, and it awarded delegate votes to Taft when no candidate had won the required 540 delegate votes. Roosevelt felt the nomination was stolen from him. Woodrow Wilson, governor of New Jersey, was the Democratic candidate. Roosevelt was unwilling to give up and decided to run for president as a third-party candidate. He and his supporters formed the Progressive Party. After he told a reporter he was "fit as a bull moose" to be president, the party became known as the Bull Moose Party.

The campaign was fierce. Wilson's New Freedom policies were even more progressive than Roosevelt's. Wilson attacked Roosevelt for his acceptance of monopolies, and Roosevelt attacked Wilson for being out of date. The campaign became a fight between Wilson and Roosevelt, and Taft was largely ignored.

Roosevelt gives a campaign speech in New Jersey in September 1912.

While Roosevelt was giving a speech on the campaign trail in October, a would-be assassin shot Roosevelt in the chest. Roosevelt's fifty-page speech and a metal eyeglasses case in his jacket saved him

by absorbing most of the bullet's impact. Bleeding from the wound, Roosevelt addressed voters anyway. He didn't want to disappoint the thousands who'd come to hear him speak. He showed them his bloody shirt and announced, "It takes more than that to kill a Bull Moose." Though he warned he couldn't speak for long, he ended up talking for more than an hour. The bullet that hit Roosevelt lodged in his rib cage. Doctors decided it would be too dangerous to remove it and left it there for the rest of his life.

The would-be assassin, John Flammang Schrank, later explained that he shot Roosevelt because he opposed third terms for presidents. He also said that the ghost of McKinley had told him to do it. Doctors declared Schrank insane, and he spent the rest of his life in a mental hospital.

ROOSEVELT'S BULLY PULPIT

Known for his colorful language, Roosevelt was famous for using the phrase "bully pulpit." At that time, *bully* meant "first-rate." *Pulpit* described a preaching position. When Roosevelt used the phrase, he meant that his place in US politics gave him an excellent forum for speaking out publicly and addressing the issues of the day. Roosevelt first used the phrase "bully pulpit" to describe how he spoke out from the White House. "I suppose my critics will call that preaching, but I have got such a bully pulpit!" he said. This term is still used today to describe the power of the president to sway public opinion.

Roosevelt's dramatic effort demonstrated his strength and vitality to the public, but it wasn't enough. Wilson won the 1912 election and become the twenty-eighth US president.

SURVIVING BRAZIL

Shortly after Wilson took office, in 1913, Roosevelt had an opportunity to go on another expedition. This time, he would explore Brazil's River of Doubt with famous Brazilian explorer Colonel Candido Mariano da Silva Rondon. The opportunity was too good to pass up. Roosevelt took Kermit along and joined a party of several expert explorers and naturalists, but compared with his African safari, the trip did not go well.

Travel through Brazil's rain forest was dangerous. Within the first few months, one person drowned and the group began to

Roosevelt explored the rain forest of Brazil in 1913. The trip was dangerous and took a toll on Roosevelt's health.

run low on supplies. Jungle insects were so fierce they ate away part of Roosevelt's helmet. Finally, Roosevelt and his son became sick with malaria.

Although he was ill, Roosevelt refused to rest for long. Working to free a trapped canoe, he cut his leg badly and developed an infection. From there, his health quickly deteriorated. As the expedition became more dangerous, Roosevelt knew he couldn't continue. He told his son to leave him to die, so he wouldn't be a burden and endanger Kermit's life.

Roosevelt had planned ahead for such a situation. He carried with him a lethal dose of morphine that he planned to ingest once Kermit left. But his son refused to leave him, and that left Roosevelt no choice but to go on. Lying under a tent in a canoe, he was feverish, helpless, and delirious. Another member of the expedition performed primitive surgery on Roosevelt's leg.

When the group finally made it out of the rain forest, Roosevelt was still alive. In his honor, the Brazilian government renamed the River of Doubt the Roosevelt River.

AFTER THE TRIP

Roosevelt's trip through Brazil left him with lasting health issues, but the legacy of the trip was also historic. After it had been explored, the area was mapped for the first time. The expedition also collected two thousand species of birds and five hundred mammals for study. In 1914 Roosevelt wrote and published a book about his experiences in Brazil called *Through the Brazilian Wilderness*.

ROOSEVELT'S FINAL YEARS

After the trip, Roosevelt was no longer the strong and resilient public figure Americans remembered. He had lost 55 pounds (25 kilograms) and was noticeably frail. He limped and leaned on a cane he jokingly called his big stick. Although he recovered, Roosevelt suffered from recurring malaria for the rest of his life.

In 1916 friends encouraged Roosevelt to run for president again. He considered the idea but eventually decided against it. Instead, he went to New Mexico and campaigned for Republican candidate Charles E. Hughes, who lost to President Woodrow Wilson.

In 1917 the United States entered World War I (1914–1918). Roosevelt went to visit President Wilson hoping to play a role in the battles overseas. His organization of the Rough Riders during the Spanish-American War had been a legendary success. Roosevelt wanted to do it again, organizing another group of volunteers and leading them in World War I.

To Roosevelt's dismay, Wilson turned him down. By now, Roosevelt was close to sixty years old and, because of his Brazilian expedition, he was also in poor health. And he didn't have experience in or knowledge of modern military operations. Nevertheless, Wilson's refusal of Roosevelt's offer hurt him deeply. Roosevelt had one other option left. While watching from the sidelines, he could still contribute to the war effort through his sons: Theodore Jr., Quentin, Kermit, and Archibald. Roosevelt had instilled his sense of duty and patriotism in his children. Though he couldn't fight himself, his sons all enlisted in the military.

Roosevelt had relished his experiences on the battlefield, but he was torn apart when Archibald and Theodore Jr. were both injured in battle. Then, on July 14, 1918, Quentin, a pilot in the US Air Service, was killed when Germans shot down his plane.

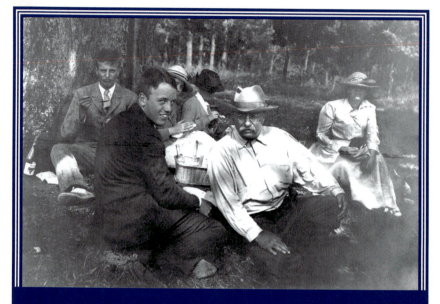

Quentin Roosevelt (front left) enlisted in the US Air Service during World War I. He was killed in combat in 1918.

Roosevelt was devastated. He continued to tell the media he was proud of Quentin and all his sons for serving the United States and the world, but Roosevelt never fully recovered from the death of his youngest son.

After the war ended with a victory for the United States and its allies, Roosevelt still hoped to regain political power. But in 1918, he had surgery that left him deaf in one ear. The same year, he was hospitalized for inflammatory rheumatism. He also disclosed a fact he'd been hiding for years: he'd been blind in one eye since boxing with a White House military aide in 1905.

On January 6, 1919, Roosevelt unexpectedly died in his sleep from a blood clot at the age of sixty. Archibald's telegram to his brothers read, "The old lion is dead." Vice President Thomas Marshall summed up Roosevelt's personality when he told the newspapers, "Death had to take him sleeping, for if Roosevelt had been awake, there would have been a fight."

ROOSEVELT'S LEGACY

Roosevelt changed the United States and the office of the presidency forever. During the nineteenth century, Congress had more power than the president. Roosevelt refused to be kept in the background and aggressively pursued an agenda of reform. By the time he left office, he had significantly expanded the role of the president. US presidents following him had more power to make decisions and drive change.

Roosevelt's domestic reforms and foreign policies also altered the country and its standing in the world. By regulating

Roosevelt in the library of his home in Oyster Bay, New York, in 1912

big business, Roosevelt made sure business owners were held accountable to society. He achieved a long-held dream of leaders and business owners when he established the Panama Canal, which permanently changed maritime travel and shipping. By building up the military and negotiating peace between other nations, he established the United States as a global power willing and able to police the rest of the world.

Although Roosevelt was a proponent of equal opportunity and championed the underdogs of society, his expansion of the Chinese Exclusion Act constrained civil rights and created a model for more immigration restrictions. Future restrictions inspired by the Chinese Exclusion Act singled out other cultures and ethnicities, including the Japanese, Middle Easterners, East Indians, and Hindus. And some of Roosevelt's policies ultimately ignored the rights of American Indians.

Roosevelt's decision in the Brownsville Affair also hurt many individuals. The incident was not examined again until nearly seventy years later, when the US Army investigated the case and granted retroactive honorable discharges to the men involved. But the repercussions of Roosevelt's action could not be reversed, and only one serviceman was still alive to receive the pension he'd earned.

As a conservationist, Roosevelt used his power to create policies others could build on. By the time he left office, he'd preserved more than 230 million acres (93 million hectares) of land, including 150 national forests, fifty-one federal bird reservations, four national game preserves, eighteen national monuments, and five national parks. He conserved the land during his lifetime and ensured that natural resources would be around for future generations to use and enjoy.

Born with both advantages and disadvantages in life, Roosevelt was a man who never lacked strength of will. He

used his charisma to win over the American people and his aggressive nature to shape the country to his standards and principles. Challenging many values, customs, traditions, and habits of his time, Roosevelt left his unique mark on the changing country.

TIMELINE

1858   Theodore Roosevelt is born on October 27.

1884   Roosevelt's daughter Alice is born on February 12. Roosevelt's mother, Mittie, and wife Alice both die on February 14.

1886   Roosevelt marries Edith Carow on December 2.

1895   Roosevelt becomes the New York City police commissioner.

1898   Roosevelt organizes the Rough Riders to fight in the Spanish-American War.

1901   US president William McKinley is assassinated. Vice President Roosevelt becomes president on September 14.

1902   Roosevelt files suit against the Northern Securities Company under the Sherman Anti-Trust Act.

The Anthracite Coal Strike begins in May, and Roosevelt is involved in negotiations between the miners and mine owners.

1904   Roosevelt is elected to a second term as president.

1905   Roosevelt helps negotiate peace between Japan and Russia to end the Russo-Japanese War.

1906   The Pure Food and Drug Act and Federal Meat Inspection Act are passed on June 30.

Roosevelt becomes the first president to travel outside the United States when he inspects the Panama Canal. The president wins the Nobel Peace Prize for helping to end the Russo-Japanese War.

1907   The Great White Fleet begins its world tour.

1912   Roosevelt campaigns and loses the presidential election to Woodrow Wilson.

1913–1914   Roosevelt explores Brazil's River of Doubt and barely survives the expedition.

1917   The United States enters World War I.

1918   Roosevelt's son Quentin is killed in battle on July 14.

1919   Roosevelt dies in his sleep on January 6.

SOURCE NOTES

10 Nathan Miller, *Theodore Roosevelt: A Life*, New York: William Morrow and Company, 1992, 36.

11 Theodore Roosevelt, "Washington's Forgotten Maxim," *Proceedings—United States Naval Institute*, Annapolis, MD: US Naval Institute, 1873, 449–450.

13 Miller, *Theodore Roosevelt*, 46.

14 Ibid., 49.

14 Ibid., 81.

15 Ibid., 89.

15 Ibid., 95–97.

17 "Theodore Roosevelt Diaries," *Library of Congress*, Accessed August 24, 2015, http://lcweb2.loc.gov/ammem/trhtml/trdiary3.html.

19 *Appleton's Annual Cyclopaedia and Register of Important Events of the Year 1902*, New York: D. Appleton and Company, 1903, 152–153.

29 "Theodore Roosevelt, 25th Vice President (1901)," *United States Senate*, Accessed August 24, 2015, http://www.senate.gov /artandhistory/history/common/generic/VP_Theodore_ Roosevelt.htm.

31 Murat Halstead, *The Life of Theodore Roosevelt*, Akron, OH: The Saalfield Publishing Co., 1902, 259.

37 George Grant, *The Life of Theodore Roosevelt*, Nashville: Cumberland House Publishing, 2005, 72.

38 Patricia O'Toole, *When Trumpets Call: Theodore Roosevelt After the White House*, New York: Simon & Schuster, 2006, 86.

46 Adam Cohen, "100 Years Later, the Food Industry is still 'The Jungle'," *The New York Times*, January 2, 2007, Accessed August 24, 2015, http://www.nytimes.com/2007/01/02/opinion /02tue4.html?_r=1&.

48 "A Brief History of Early Drug Regulation in the United States," *Society of Toxology*, Accessed August 25, 2015, http://www .toxicology.org/about/history/docs/poster_ToxTimeline.pdf.

48   Ibid.

49   Theodore Roosevelt, *Addresses and Presidential Messages of Theodore Roosevelt, 1902–1904,* New York: G.P. Putnam & Sons, 1904, 349.

50   Theodore Roosevelt, "Speak Softly . . .," *Library of Congress,* Accessed August 25, 2015, http://www.loc.gov/exhibits/treasures/trm139.html.

56   Theodore Roosevelt, "The Nobel Peace Prize 1906: Acceptance Speech," *The Official Web Site of the Nobel Prize,* Accessed August 25, 2015, http://www.nobelprize.org/nobel_prizes/peace/laureates/1906/roosevelt-acceptance.html.

62   Gardiner Harris. "The Underside of the Welcome Mat." *The New York Times,* November 8, 2008. Accessed August 25, 2015. http://www.nytimes.com/2008/11/09/weekinreview/09harris.html?ref=politics&_r=0

62   H.W. Brands, "Commentary: When a Black Man was Invited to the White House for Dinner," *CNN,* November 10, 2008, Accessed August 25, 2015, http://edition.cnn.com/2008/POLITICS/11/06/brands.booker.theodore/index.html?iref=topnews.

65   Robert Cornelius V. Meyers, *Theodore Roosevelt, Patriot and Statesman: the True Story of an Ideal American,* Philadelphia: P.W. Zeigler & Co., 1902, 445.

67   Theodore Roosevelt, "Kidd's 'Social Evolution'," *The North American Review, Volume 161,* New York: No. 3 East Fourteenth St., 1895, 109.

69   "Roosevelt Centre of Suffrage Host," the *New York Times,* May 3, 1913, Accessed August 25, 2015, http://query.nytimes.com/mem/archive-free/pdf?res=9404E1D9173FE633A25750C0A9639C946296D6CF.

70   Miller, *Theodore Roosevelt,* 466.

72   Miller, *Theodore Roosevelt,* 380–381.

76   J. Lee Thompson, *Theodore Roosevelt Abroad: Nature, Empire, and the Journey of an American President,* New York: Palgrave Macmillan, 2013, 56.

77 Paul Russell Cutright, *Theodore Roosevelt: The Making of a Conservationist*, Chicago: University of Illinois Press, 1985, 211.

80 Theodore Roosevelt, "Theodore Roosevelt 'Conservation as a National Duty,' May 13, 1908," *Voices of Democracy: The US Oratory Project*, Accessed August 26, 2015, http://voicesofdemocracy .umd.edu/theodore-roosevelt-conservation-as-a-national-duty -speech-text/.

81 Treadwell Cleveland, Jr., "The North American Conservation Conference," *Conservation: Official Magazine of the American Forestry Association*, Vol. XV, No. 1. January 1909, 159.

83 Kent Garber, "Teddy Roosevelt, on the Bull Moose Party Ticket, Battles Incumbent William Howard Taft," *U.S. News & World Report*, January 17, 2008, Accessed August 26, 2015, http://www .usnews.com/news/articles/2008/01/17/three-way-race-of-1912 -had-it-all.

85 Ibid.

86 Mara Bovsun, "Justice Story: Teddy Roosevelt Survives Assassin When Bullet Hits Folded Speech in His Pocket," *New York Daily News*, March 12, 2013, Accessed August 26, 2015, http://www .nydailynews.com/news/justice-story/takes-kill-bull-moose -article-1.1179536.

86 Paul Dickson, *Words from the White House*, New York: Walker Publishing Co., 2013, 41.

90 Edward J. Renehan, Jr., *The Lion's Pride: Theodore Roosevelt and His Family in Peace and War*, New York: Oxford University Press, 1998, 222.

91 Ibid.

GLOSSARY

barracks: buildings where soldiers live

conservation: the protection of animals, plants, and natural resources

consumer: a person who buys goods and services

corruption: dishonest or unethical behavior, especially by those in power

discriminatory: unfair, and often based on a person's gender, race, or ethnicity

maritime: of or relating to the sea

pension: an amount of money or payments made by a company or the government to individuals who are no longer working

philanthropist: a wealthy person who uses money and other resources to help others

rebate: a refund on a payment

segregation: a system of separating different races from one another

Socialist: a person who advocates for an economic system in which industry and the production of goods are controlled by a central government

suffrage: the right to vote

telegram: a message sent over wires by telegraph

volatile: unpredictable and dangerous

SELECTED BIBLIOGRAPHY

"Adirondack Journal—an Adirondack Presidential History." Adirondack Museum. Accessed August 26, 2015. http://www.adkmuseum.org/about_us/adirondack_journal/?id=117.

"The Author." Theodore Roosevelt Association. Accessed August 26, 2015. http://www.theodoreroosevelt.org/site/c.elKSIdOWIiJ8H/b.8344387/k.2C4D/The_AUTHOR.htm.

Cutright, Paul Russell. *Theodore Roosevelt: The Making of a Conservationist.* Chicago: University of Illinois Press, 1985.

"The Life of Theodore Roosevelt." National Park Service. Accessed August 26, 2015. http://www.nps.gov/thri/theodorerooseveltbio.htm.

Miller, Nathan. *Theodore Roosevelt: A Life.* New York: William Morrow, 1992.

Roosevelt, Theodore. *Addresses and Presidential Messages of Theodore Roosevelt, 1902–1904.* New York: G. P. Putnam's Sons, 1904.

"Theodore Roosevelt." Miller Center, University of Virginia. Accessed August 26, 2015. http://millercenter.org/president/roosevelt.

"Theodore Roosevelt Timeline." National Park Service. Accessed August 26, 2015. http://www.nps.gov/thro/historyculture/theodore-roosevelt-timeline.htm.

Thompson, Lee. *Theodore Roosevelt Abroad: Nature, Empire, and the Journey of an American President.* New York: Palgrave Macmillan, 2013.

"T.R. the Rough Rider: Hero of the Spanish-American War." National Park Service. Accessed August 26, 2015. http://www.nps.gov/thrb/historyculture/tr-rr-spanamwar.htm.

"TR: The Story of Theodore Roosevelt." *American Experience, PBS.* Accessed August 26, 2015. http://www.pbs.org/wgbh/americanexperience/features/introduction/tr-introduction/.

FURTHER INFORMATION

Biddulph, Stephen G. *Five Old Men of Yellowstone: The Rise of Interpretation in the First National Park*. Salt Lake City: University of Utah Press, 2013.
Find out more about the nation's first national park.

Brill, Marlene Targ. *America in the 1900s*. Minneapolis: Twenty-First Century Books, 2010.
Learn about life in the United States while Roosevelt was president.

Cooper, Michael L. *Theodore Roosevelt: A Twentieth-Century Life*. New York: Viking, 2009.
Check out this book for more on Roosevelt's exciting life.

Garraty, John A. *Theodore Roosevelt: American Rough Rider*. New York: Sterling, 2007.
Learn more about Roosevelt's Rough Riders during the Spanish-American War.

Marrin, Albert. *The Great Adventure: Theodore Roosevelt and the Rise of Modern America*. New York: Dutton, 2007.
Learn about Roosevelt's life and political career in this book.

National Park Service
http://www.nps.gov/index.htm
Visit this site for information about the United States' national monuments, national parks, and more.

Richards, Marlee. *America in the 1910s*. Minneapolis: Twenty-First Century Books, 2010.
Learn more about life during Roosevelt's time.

Smithsonian—Presidents in Waiting
http://www.npg.si.edu/exhibit/VicePres/index.html
Visit this site to learn about Roosevelt and other vice presidents who rose to become US presidents.

The White House—Theodore Roosevelt
https://www.whitehouse.gov/1600/presidents/theodoreroosevelt
Learn about Theodore Roosevelt, the twenty-sixth US president, on this site.

INDEX

PHOTO ACKNOWLEDGMENTS

The images in this book are used with the permission of: © iStockphoto.com/hudiemm (sunburst); © iStockphoto.com/Nic_Taylor (parchment); © iStockphoto.com/Phil Cardamone, (bunting); Letter from Roosevelt to Lincoln, Courtesy of The Abraham Lincoln Papers at the Library of Congress, p. 2 (background); Library of Congress, pp. 2, 6, 9, 15, 18, 23, 25, 32, 35, 37, 40, 42, 44, 51, 58, 62, 63, 69, 85, 91; Fine Arts Library, Harvard University, p. 11; Houghton Library, Harvard University, pp. 12, 14, 21, 27, 70, 73, 83; © iStockphoto.com/elgol, p. 28; © Corbis, pp. 29, 47, 54, 77, 90; © Universal History Archive/UIG/Getty Images, p. 34; © Universal History Archive/Getty Images, p. 45; © Hulton-Deutsch Collection/Corbis, p. 46; © Laura Westlund/Independent Picture Service, pp. 53, 74; © Hulton Archive/Getty Images, p. 56; © David J. & Janice L. Frent Collection/Corbis, p. 61; © Underwood & Underwood/Corbis, pp. 64, 80, 87; Schomburg Center For Research In Black Culture, Manuscripts, Archives And Rare Books Division, Picture Collection, The Branch Libraries, The New York Public Library, Astor, Lenox and Tilden Foundations, p. 67; © US Army/National Archives/The LIFE Picture Collection/Getty Images, p. 68; Acme Roto Service/Independent Picture Service, p. 75; © A.A.M. Van der Heyden/Independent Picture Service, p. 76; © Ron Chapple/Dreamstime.com, p. 84.

Front cover: Letter from Roosevelt to Lincoln, Courtesy of The Abraham Lincoln Papers at the Library of Congress; portrait and signature courtesy of the Library of Congress; © iStockphoto.com/WilshireImages (flag bunting).

Back cover: © iStockphoto.com/hudiemm (sunburst); © iStockphoto.com/Nic_Taylor (parchment).

ABOUT THE AUTHOR

Heather E. Schwartz is a journalist and writer. She is the author of more than fifty nonfiction children's titles and has written articles for *National Geographic Kids* and *Discovery Girls*. Schwartz lives in New York.